The Self-love Workbook for Teens

Build Confidence, Eliminate Self-Doubt and Treat Yourself With Kindness

Bella Clark

Copyright © 2023 by Bella Clark

First edition

A FREE GIFT TO OUR READERS!

Printable Journal With Daily Prompts

Get your free gift here:

Table of Contents

Introduction

Like a tree that starts as a tiny seed and grows into a majestic plant, self-love begins as a small seed within us and blossoms into a beautiful relationship with ourselves. As teenagers, we often face challenges and hardships that can make it difficult to love ourselves. Whether it's the pressure to fit in, the stress of school or relationships, or just the ups and downs of growing up, it's easy to forget to take care of ourselves and our emotional wellbeing.

This is where our workbook on self-love comes in. Similarly to the nurture required to planting and growing a tree, this workbook will guide you on your journey towards developing a strong sense of self-love. Like a tree that encounters harsh weather and conditions, you will learn how to care for yourself throughout the hardships you may face. Through the chapters of this book, you will discover practical ways to nurture your self-love, including self-reflection exercises, tips for self-care, and strategies for building self-esteem.

Remember, just like a tree needs regular care and attention to grow strong and healthy, so too does your self-love. With dedication, patience, and the tools provided in this workbook, you can cultivate a deep and meaningful relationship with yourself. So, let's get started on this journey of self-discovery and growth together!

What Exactly Is Self-love?

Self-love is like having a BFF, but that BFF is actually you! It means treating yourself with kindness and respect, just like you would with your best friend. It means not being too hard on yourself, forgiving yourself when you make mistakes, and taking care of your mental and physical health.

Now, let's talk about some situations where you might not love yourself.

- Have you ever looked in the mirror and wished you looked like someone else?
- Have you ever been afraid to speak up because you were worried people might judge you?
- Have you ever put yourself down because of a bad grade or a mistake you made?

All of these situations can make you feel self-conscious and like you don't love yourself. But here's the thing: you're not alone. Every teenager goes through moments of self-doubt and insecurity.

The good news is that there are things you can do to boost your self-love. Surround yourself with positive people who lift you up, focus on your strengths and accomplishments, practice self-care like taking a bubble bath or going for a walk, and remind yourself that you are worthy of love and respect.
So remember, being your own BFF is the best thing you can do for yourself. Treat yourself with kindness and respect, and watch your self-love grow!

In the next chapters, we'll explore techniques to help you love yourself more. You are worthy of love and respect, so let's work on building that self-love!

How to Use

This workbook is designed to guide you through the process of achieving self-love. The workbook is divided into four chapters, each representing a different phase in the lifecycle of a tree: Seed, Birth, and Juvenile, all leading to the final chapter, Adult.

Throughout the four chapters, you will learn skills and exercises that will help you move forward towards creating the best relationship with yourself and reaching self-love. As a teenager, this is a crucial time in your life to learn and practice self-love.

As you progress through the workbook, take your time and don't rush. Remember, self-love is a journey, and it takes time and effort to cultivate. This workbook is designed to guide you through the process, but ultimately, it's up to you to put in the work and make the changes necessary to achieve self-love. Good luck on your journey!

How to Use

Seed: You're Beginning Your Journey

In this chapter, you will learn how to plant the seeds of self-love. You will learn about the importance of self-awareness, how to recognize and address negative self-talk, and how to set healthy boundaries. This phase is all about self-discovery and planting the seeds that will eventually grow into self-love.

Birth: The First Sprouts of Self-love

In this chapter, you will begin to see the first sprouts of self-love. You will learn about the importance of self-care and how to practice it in your everyday life. You will also learn about gratitude and how it can help shift your mindset towards positivity.

Juvenile: Self-love Grows Stronger

In this chapter, you will see your self-love continue to grow stronger. You will learn about the power of self-talk and how to speak positively to yourself. You will also learn about self-confidence and how to build it up.

Adult: Self-love Unlocked

In this final chapter, you will reach the goal of self-love. You will learn how to maintain a positive relationship with yourself and how to continue to practice self-love throughout your life. You will also learn about the benefits of self-love and how it can improve your overall well-being.

Quiz: Which Phase of the Cycle Do You Find Yourself In?

It is time for us to see which phase you are at right now. Please give a score from 1-10 on how much you agree with each statement, where 1 means strongly disagree and 10 means strongly agree.

I am comfortable with my own strengths and weaknesses.
Strongly disagree 1   2   3   4   5   6   7   8   9   10 Strongly agree

I feel confident expressing my opinions and ideas.
Strongly disagree 1   2   3   4   5   6   7   8   9   10 Strongly agree

I make time for self-care activities that benefit my mental health and well-being.
Strongly disagree 1   2   3   4   5   6   7   8   9   10 Strongly agree

I am able to handle stress and difficult situations effectively.
Strongly disagree 1   2   3   4   5   6   7   8   9   10 Strongly agree

I am open-minded and respectful towards people with different beliefs and perspectives.
Strongly disagree 1   2   3   4   5   6   7   8   9   10 Strongly agree

I have a good support system of family and friends that I can rely on when needed.
Strongly disagree 1   2   3   4   5   6   7   8   9   10 Strongly agree

I am motivated and committed to achieving my goals.
Strongly disagree 1   2   3   4   5   6   7   8   9   10 Strongly agree

I am responsible with my time and prioritize my tasks and responsibilities effectively.
Strongly disagree 1   2   3   4   5   6   7   8   9   10 Strongly agree

I have good communication skills and am able to express my thoughts and feelings clearly.
Strongly disagree 1   2   3   4   5   6   7   8   9   10 Strongly agree

I am able to learn from my mistakes and use them as opportunities for growth and improvement.
Strongly disagree 1   2   3   4   5   6   7   8   9   10 Strongly agree

Remember, this is just a self-assessment exercise and it's okay if you don't score high on every statement. Use this as an opportunity to reflect on areas where you may want to improve and set goals to work towards becoming the best version of yourself.

Self-Awareness Superstar

Scores: 8-10 on most statements
You have a high level of self-awareness and are in tune with your emotions, strengths, and areas for growth. You have a positive self-image and are able to communicate effectively with others. Keep up the great work!

Goal-Getter

Scores: 6-8 on most statements
You are a motivated individual with goals in mind, but may struggle with some aspects of self-care or handling stress. You have strong communication skills and a supportive network, which can help you achieve your aspirations with focus and dedication.

Growth Mindset Guru

Scores: 4-6 on most statements
You may have some challenges in certain areas of your life, but you are committed to learning and growing. You understand the importance of self-care and have good communication skills, but may need to work on building your support system or developing more effective strategies for handling stress.

Reflection Rookie

Scores: 1-4 on most statements
You may be struggling with self-awareness or have difficulty communicating effectively with others. However, the fact that you completed this assessment shows a willingness to reflect and improve. In this workbook you will find resources to help you develop these important life skills.

Seed: You're Beginning Your Journey

Just like a seed that grows into a tree, you too have the potential to grow and blossom into the best version of yourself. This chapter will guide you on the path to discovering your own unique identity, helping you to appreciate and love yourself for who you are.

In this chapter, you will discover techniques and exercises that will help you to get to know yourself better. Through self-reflection and exploration, you will learn more about your personality, values, beliefs, and strengths. You will also explore the things that make you feel happy, fulfilled, and content. These discoveries will help you to gain a better understanding of who you are, which is an important step towards cultivating self-love.

We will also explore techniques that will help you to learn to love yourself. You will learn how to practice self-compassion, how to challenge negative self-talk, and how to cultivate positive affirmations. You will also discover the importance of self-care and how to prioritize your physical, emotional, and mental well-being.

Just like planting and nurturing a seed, cultivating self-love takes time, patience, and effort. But with the right techniques and mindset, you can grow into the best version of yourself. Let's begin this journey of self-discovery and self-love together.

WHO AM I?

In this chapter, we will explore the concept of self-identity and help you get to know yourself better. As a teenager, you may be going through a period of change and growth, and it's important to understand who you are at your core. By asking yourself questions and reflecting on your perceptions of yourself, you can gain a deeper understanding of your personality, beliefs, values, and strengths. So, let's dive in and begin this journey of self-discovery together!

⭘ How do you feel about yourself when you look in the mirror?

_____

_____

_____

_____

_____

⭘ Are you kind and compassionate to yourself, or do you often criticize yourself?

_____

_____

_____

_____

_____

O Do you find it easy to forgive yourself when you make a mistake, or do you hold onto feelings of guilt and shame?

_____

_____

_____

_____

_____

O How do you treat others when you are feeling low or insecure about yourself?

_____

_____

_____

_____

_____

O Are you able to recognize your strengths and weaknesses, or do you only focus on your flaws?

_____

_____

_____

_____

_____

O How do you respond to criticism from others?

_____

_____

_____

_____

_____

9

○ Do you feel comfortable setting boundaries with others when you need to protect your own well-being?

_____

_____

_____

_____

_____

○ How do you react when someone disagrees with you or has a different perspective?

_____

_____

_____

_____

○ Are you able to express your emotions and needs in a healthy way, or do you tend to suppress them?

_____

_____

_____

_____

○ How do you prioritize self-care and self-love in your daily life?

_____

_____

_____

_____

Reflection

Now it's time for you to reflect on the answers to these questions. Take a moment to consider whether your responses were mostly positive or negative. If you found that you had a lot of negative responses, it's important to explore why that might be.

Think about what exactly makes you react negatively in certain situations, and try to identify how that could be related to the way you feel about yourself.

Perhaps you noticed that you often criticize yourself, which may stem from a lack of self-esteem. Or, maybe you struggle to set boundaries with others because you fear rejection or don't value your own needs. By understanding the underlying reasons behind your negative reactions, you can start to address them and cultivate more self-love and compassion.

Remember, self-love is a journey, and it takes time and effort to develop. But by being aware of your thoughts and behaviors, and making a conscious effort to treat yourself with kindness and respect, you can start to build a healthier relationship with yourself and those around you.

FOCUS ON YOUR TARGET

The teenage years can be a period of great change and growth, and it's important to take the time to concentrate on yourself and your personal development. Self-love is a crucial component of this process, but it can be difficult to know where to begin or what your ultimate goal should be.

In this chapter, we will help you identify what you want to achieve through self-love and provide you with actionable steps to reach your target. So take a deep breath, clear your mind, and let's begin the journey of self-discovery together.

O What makes me truly happy and fulfilled in life?

_____

_____

_____

_____

_____

O What are my natural strengths and talents, and how can I use them to make a positive impact on the world??

_____

_____

_____

_____

_____

○ What are the values that are most important to me, and how can I align my goals with these values?

_____

_____

_____

_____

_____

○ What fears or insecurities are holding me back from pursuing my dreams, and how can I overcome them?

_____

_____

_____

_____

_____

○ Where do I see myself in 5, 10, or 20 years from now, and what steps can I take today to make that vision a reality?

_____

_____

_____

_____

_____

13

"FEEL GOOD" PLAYLIST

This exercise will help you feel good, and it's all about creating your own feel-good playlist. Positivity is essential for a happy and healthy life, and music is a powerful tool to help you achieve that. When you listen to music that you love, it can shift your mood, make you feel energized, and even reduce stress levels.

This exercise is all about identifying songs that put you in a good mood and creating a playlist that you can turn to whenever you need a pick-me-up. You will have the freedom to choose any type of music that resonates with you, and the songs can be old or new. The only requirement is that they make you feel good!

In a world where we are constantly exposed to negativity and stress, it's important to prioritize our mental health and well-being. By taking the time to create a feel-good playlist, you are making a conscious effort to surround yourself with positivity and joy. So, grab your headphones, turn up the volume, and let's get started on creating your own personal feel-good playlist!

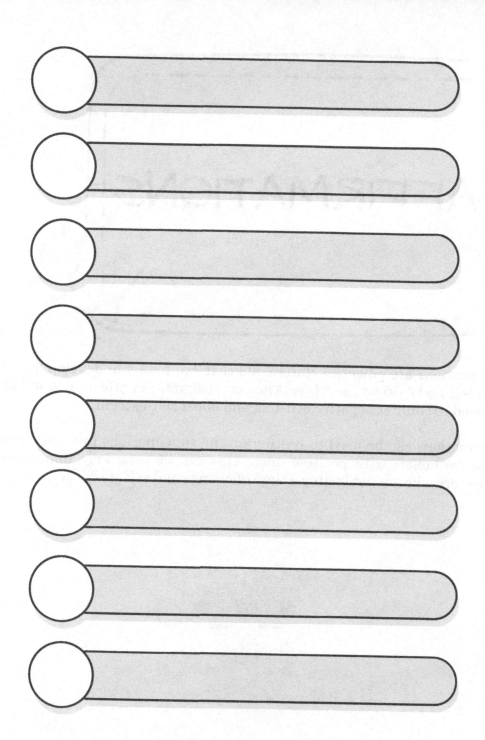

AFFIRMATIONS

Affirmations are powerful statements that can help you develop a positive mindset and cultivate self-love. They are a simple yet effective tool that can be used to counter negative self-talk and boost self-esteem.

Affirmations can be used to reprogram the subconscious mind and replace negative beliefs with positive ones. This can be especially important for teenagers who are navigating a time of change and self-discovery.

Here are some examples that you can start using daily:

I am worthy of love and respect.

I choose to see the good in myself and others.

I am confident in who I am.

I deserve happiness and success.

I am strong and capable of overcoming any challenge.

I trust myself to make the wisest decisions for my life.

I am beautiful/handsome just the way I am.

I am deserving of love and affection.

I am loved and supported by the people around me.

I am grateful for my strengths and weaknesses.

I choose to forgive myself and others for mistakes.

I trust the journey of my life and know that everything will work out for the best.

I am enough just as I am.

I am worthy of pursuing my dreams and passions.

I am proud of who I am becoming.

Writing your own affirmations is a great way to personalize this practice and connect with yourself on a deeper level.

Think about an area of your life where you struggle with negative self-talk or lack of confidence. It could be related to school, relationships, or something else. Write down a few affirmations that directly address those negative thoughts or feelings. For example, if you struggle with feeling inadequate in school, you could write an affirmation like "I am capable of learning and growing every day."

Make sure to use positive language and focus on what you want to believe about yourself. Repeat these affirmations to yourself daily and notice how they make you feel. Over time, you may find that your mindset shifts towards a more positive and loving view of yourself.

Write your own affirmations:

_____

_____

_____

_____

_____

_____

_____

_____

_____

_____

_____

_____

WHEN DID YOU EXPERIENCE SELF-LOVE?

Set aside some quiet time for yourself to reflect on your past experiences. Find a comfortable and quiet space where you won't be interrupted.

Take a few deep breaths and try to relax your mind and body. You might want to close your eyes or focus on a calming object.

Begin to recall times when you felt really good about yourself. These could be any experiences, big or small, that made you feel proud, happy, or accomplished. It could be a personal achievement, a kind act you did for someone else, a compliment you received, or anything else that made you feel good.

Write down each situation in a list format, including as much detail as possible about what happened, how you felt, and why it made you feel good.

Self-love experiences

☐ _____
☐ _____
☐ _____
☐ _____
☐ _____
☐ _____
☐ _____
☐ _____
☐ _____
☐ _____

Once you have listed 10 situations, take some time to reflect on them. Notice any patterns or themes that emerge. What do these situations have in common? Are there any recurring emotions or experiences that made you feel good?

Use this exercise as an opportunity to celebrate yourself and acknowledge your strengths. You might even want to create a gratitude list of all the positive qualities and experiences you have had in your life.

Remember, self-love and self-appreciation is important, so make sure to take some time for yourself and reflect on your accomplishments and positive experiences. This exercise can help you to develop a more positive self-image and build your self-esteem.

MIRROR REFLECTION

One of the self-love exercises that can help you boost your self-confidence and self-esteem is writing positive messages to yourself and sticking them to your mirror.

The first step of this exercise is to think of positive affirmations that resonate with you. These affirmations can be simple statements such as "I am capable," "I am enough," "I am worthy," or anything that makes you feel good about yourself. Once you have come up with your affirmations, write them on sticky notes or colorful pieces of paper.

The next step is to stick these notes to your mirror, where you can see them every morning when you get ready for the day. By doing so, you are creating a habit of reinforcing positive self-talk and building a positive self-image. Whenever you look at yourself in the mirror, you will be reminded of your worth and potential.

Seeing positive messages in the mirror is important because it is tied to the image of self. It can change the way you perceive yourself, your abilities, and your worth. By repeating these affirmations, you are training your mind to think positively about yourself, which can have a profound impact on your mental health and overall wellbeing.

By doing this exercise, you are taking a step towards self-love and self-acceptance. So, be patient with yourself and keep practicing. You are worthy of love and respect, and you deserve to treat yourself with kindness and compassion.

COUNTER ARGUMENTS

Think back on three situations in your life where you felt unworthy or bad with yourself. It could be anything from a social situation to a school assignment to a relationship with a friend or family member.

For each situation, write down your thoughts at the time. What were you telling yourself? What were the negative self-talk or beliefs you had about yourself? Write these down as specifically and honestly as possible.

○ **Situation 1**

_____

_____

_____

_____

_____

_____

○ **Situation 2**

_____

_____

_____

_____

_____

◯ Situation 3

_____

_____

_____

_____

_____

_____

Once you've written down your thoughts, take a moment to reflect on why you might have been feeling this way. Was there something going on in your life that was causing stress or anxiety? Did someone say or do something that hurt your feelings? Try to identify the root cause of these negative thoughts.

Next, challenge these negative thoughts. Write down counterarguments to these beliefs that are more compassionate and realistic. For example, if you wrote down "I'm so stupid" because you didn't do well on a test, write down something like "It's okay to make mistakes. Everyone has strengths and weaknesses, and I can work on improving my skills in this area."
Finally, take a moment to show yourself some self-love and kindness. Write down three things you like about yourself, and three things you're proud of. These can be small things like "I have a good sense of humor" or bigger accomplishments like "I made the varsity soccer team."

Remember, it's normal to have negative thoughts about yourself from time to time, but it's important to challenge those thoughts and treat yourself with kindness and compassion. By doing this exercise regularly, you can build self-esteem and develop a more positive self-image.

SELF-DOUBT

Did you experience self-doubt in any of the following situations?

○ When you were asked to give a speech in front of the class.

○ When you were wearing something you didn't feel comfortable in.

○ When you were starting a new school or class.

○ When you were in a new social situation with unfamiliar people.

○ When you were being teased or bullied by other teenagers.

○ When you were trying out for a sports team or auditioning for a play.

○ When you were going through a major physical change, such as puberty
.

○ When you were struggling with a particular subject in school.

○ When you were trying to make new friends or fit in with a new group of people.

○ When you were pursuing a new hobby or interest and felt unsure of yourself.

25

As you end this first phase towards self-love, it's important to remember that the journey itself is just as important as the destination.

By incorporating self-love techniques such as mirror reflection, counter arguments, and positive talk, you can cultivate a healthier and more positive relationship with yourself.

Remember that you are worthy of kindness and admiration, and that it's okay to put yourself first sometimes.

Listening to a feel-good playlist and reminding yourself of your strengths and accomplishments can go a long way towards boosting your confidence and self-esteem.

So take a deep breath, be kind to yourself, and embrace the power of self-love as you continue on your journey towards a happier, healthier, and more fulfilling life.

Birth: The First Sprouts of Self-love

By now, you've likely explored different techniques and strategies to cultivate a positive self-image, but the journey towards self-love doesn't end there. In this chapter, we'll be discussing the importance of self-care and how it plays a crucial role in nurturing the seeds of self-love that you've planted.

Self-care involves taking deliberate actions to improve your physical, emotional, and mental wellbeing. This means treating your body with kindness, setting healthy boundaries, and engaging in activities that bring you joy and fulfillment. When we neglect self-care, we're more susceptible to stress, burnout, and negative self-talk, which can hinder our ability to love ourselves fully.

We'll also be discussing the impact of self-doubt on our self-perception. Self-doubt is the voice in our head that tells us we're not good enough, smart enough, or worthy of love and success. It can be a formidable obstacle on the road to self-love, but it's important to recognize that it's normal to experience self-doubt from time to time. By understanding how it affects us and learning strategies to combat it, we can cultivate a more positive and compassionate relationship with ourselves.

So, get ready to dive deeper into the journey of self-love.

REFLECT ON YOUR POSITIVE QUALITIES

Reflect on your positive qualities. Write down all the things that you like about yourself, such as your sense of humor, your kindness, your creativity, your intelligence, your loyalty, your generosity, or your perseverance. Think about the things that make you unique and special.

- ☐ _____
- ☐ _____
- ☐ _____
- ☐ _____
- ☐ _____

- [ ] _____
- [ ] _____
- [ ] _____
- [ ] _____
- [ ] _____
- [ ] _____
- [ ] _____
- [ ] _____
- [ ] _____
- [ ] _____
- [ ] _____
- [ ] _____

WHAT DRIVES ME?

For many of us, especially as teenagers, it can be tough to stay focused on our aspirations when distractions and setbacks arise. We may feel overwhelmed, unmotivated, or unsure of our next steps.

Have you ever experienced a moment where you felt like giving up on something you wanted to achieve? Maybe you were studying for a test and felt like you weren't making progress, or you were working on a creative project and hit a roadblock. These moments can be discouraging, but it's important to remember that everyone experiences them at some point.

In this exercise, we'll take a closer look at what motivates us and how we can use that knowledge to stay driven towards our goals. By writing down what drives us, we can create a list of reminders that we can turn to when we need an extra boost of motivation. So let's get started and discover what drives you!

What drives me?

- [ ] ______________________________
- [ ] ______________________________
- [ ] ______________________________
- [ ] ______________________________
- [ ] ______________________________
- [ ] ______________________________
- [ ] ______________________________
- [ ] ______________________________
- [ ] ______________________________
- [ ] ______________________________
- [ ] ______________________________
- [ ] ______________________________

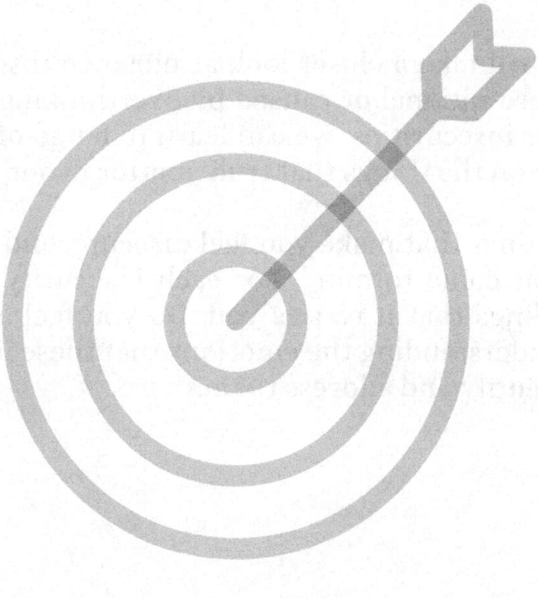

MY INSECURITIES

It's natural to have moments of doubt and insecurity as we navigate the complexities of adolescence and try to figure out who we are and where we fit in. However, it's also common to be insecure about things that, in the grand scheme of things, won't really matter in the long run.

Have you ever found yourself worrying about something that you later realized wasn't worth the stress? Perhaps you were anxious about what people thought of your outfit, or worried that you weren't popular enough. These are just a few examples of the many insecurities that can plague us as teens, but the truth is that most of them are based on overthinking or irrational fears.

In this exercise, we'll take a closer look at our own insecurities and reflect on whether they are rational or caused by overthinking. By acknowledging and examining our insecurities, we can learn to let go of the ones that don't serve us and focus on the things that truly matter in our lives.

Think about the things that make you feel insecure, and write down a list of 10 insecurities that come to mind. For each insecurity, take a moment to reflect on the feelings that it causes you. Do you feel anxious, worried, or self-conscious? Understanding the emotions that these insecurities bring up can help you to identify and address them.

MY INSECURITIES

_____

_____

_____

_____

_____

_____

_____

_____

_____

REFLECTION

We all experience moments of self-doubt and negative self-talk that can impact our mental health and well-being. In this chapter, we will explore why we feel self-doubt and how we can practice self-love to overcome negative thinking patterns.

Self-doubt can stem from several sources, such as past experiences, societal expectations, and comparisons to others. For example, you may feel insecure about your appearance because of unrealistic beauty standards perpetuated by the media or social media. Alternatively, you may have experienced failure or rejection in the past, leading you to question your abilities and worth.

The truth is that self-doubt is not grounded in reality. It's a destructive thought pattern that only serves to hold us back and prevent us from reaching our full potential. Instead of focusing on our strengths and accomplishments, we obsess over our flaws and shortcomings, leading to feelings of anxiety and low self-esteem.

It's important to remember that self-doubt is a normal part of life. Everyone experiences it at some point, and it's okay to feel unsure of yourself sometimes. The key is to practice self-love and compassion to overcome negative thinking patterns.

One way to practice self-love is to focus on your strengths and accomplishments. Celebrate your success, no matter how small, and acknowledge your hard work and effort. It's also essential to surround yourself with positive influences and people who uplift and support you.

Another way to practice self-love is to engage in activities that bring you excitement and fulfillment. Whether it's reading a book, painting, or spending time with friends and family, make time for things that make you happy and fulfilled.

Remember, self-love is not selfish. It's an essential aspect of caring for yourself and your well-being. By practicing self-love, you can break free from negative thinking patterns and cultivate a positive and confident mindset.

I

NEGATIVE SELF-TALK

We all have an inner voice that narrates our experiences and shapes our perceptions of ourselves and the world around us. However, sometimes this inner voice can be overly critical and negative, leading us to see ourselves in a bad light and hold ourselves back from reaching our full potential.

Have you ever caught yourself saying things like "I'm not good enough," "I'm such a failure," or "I'll never be able to do this"? These negative self-talk patterns can be harmful and limiting, and they're often based on unfounded beliefs and assumptions about ourselves.

In this exercise, I encourage you to take a closer look at the negative statements that you tell yourself and reflect on why they are not founded.

Write down the negative self-talk patterns that you tend to engage in and challenge them with evidence to the contrary. Use "you" to address yourself, and be kind and compassionate as you work through this exercise.
Remember, it's normal to struggle with negative self-talk from time to time, and it takes practice to reframe these patterns and build a more positive self-image. So let's get started and explore our negative self-talk together.

SELF-DOUBT QUIZ

I am always worried about what others think of me.

I find it difficult to accept compliments.

I often compare myself to others and feel like I fall short.

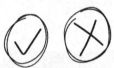

I feel like I am not good enough.

I have trouble making decisions because I am afraid of making the wrong choice.

I am afraid of trying new things because I might fail.

I often second-guess myself and doubt my abilities.

I am constantly worried about the future.

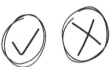

I feel like I don't belong or fit in.

I am afraid to speak up for myself and assert my opinions.

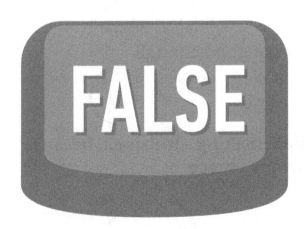

If you answered "True" to most or all of the statements: This may indicate that you struggle with self-doubt and low self-esteem. However, recognizing these thoughts and feelings is an important first step towards building self-love. You can start by acknowledging your positive qualities and achievements, practicing self-compassion, and challenging negative self-talk.

If you answered "False" to most or all of the statements: This may suggest that you have a strong sense of self-confidence and self-love. However, it is important to remember that everyone experiences self-doubt and insecurity from time to time. It is helpful to continue to practice self-compassion and positive self-talk to maintain a healthy relationship with yourself.

If you answered a mix of "True" and "False" to the statements: This may indicate that you have some areas of self-doubt and some areas of self-confidence. This is normal and okay! You can start by focusing on your strengths and achievements, and working on self-improvement in the areas that you struggle with. It is important to remember that self-love is a journey and it takes time and effort to develop a healthy relationship with yourself.

SELF-CARE FOR 5 DAYS

Self-care is the practice of taking care of your physical, mental, and emotional health. This can include things like eating healthy, getting enough sleep, exercising regularly, and taking breaks when needed. Self-care is not selfish or indulgent, but rather it's necessary for maintaining a healthy and balanced lifestyle.

Self-love is the practice of accepting and loving yourself for who you are, flaws and all. This can be a difficult concept, especially when you are constantly bombarded with messages that you need to look, act, or think a certain way. However, self-love is essential for building confidence, self-esteem, and resilience.

In this chapter, we will explore the importance of self-care and self-love, and you will practice one self-care activity for 5 days and write down how you felt afterwards to help build these practices into your daily lives.

SELF-CARE DAY 1 ♥

Self-care activity:

_____
_____
_____
_____

My feelings/thoughts before the activity:

_____
_____
_____
_____

My feelings/thoughts after the activity:

_____
_____
_____
_____

SELF-CARE
DAY 2 🩶

Self-care activity:

_____

_____

_____

_____

_____

My feelings/thoughts before the activity:

_____

_____

_____

_____

_____

My feelings/thoughts after the activity:

_____

_____

_____

_____

_____

SELF-CARE
DAY 3 ♥

Self-care activity:

_____

_____

_____

_____

My feelings/thoughts before the activity:

_____

_____

_____

_____

My feelings/thoughts after the activity:

_____

_____

_____

_____

SELF-CARE
DAY 4 ♥

Self-care activity:

_____

_____

_____

_____

My feelings/thoughts before the activity:

_____

_____

_____

_____

My feelings/thoughts after the activity:

_____

_____

_____

_____

SELF-CARE DAY 5 ♥

Self-care activity:

_____

_____

_____

_____

My feelings/thoughts before the activity:

_____

_____

_____

_____

My feelings/thoughts after the activity:

_____

_____

_____

_____

Juvenile: Self-love Grows Stronger

In the midst of adolescence challenges, it is easy to be overly self-critical and develop negative self-talk, which can affect your self-esteem and overall well-being.

By the end of this chapter, you will have a better understanding of the importance of positive self-talk and self-compassion in building a healthy relationship with yourself. You will learn that self-love is not a one-time event but a continuous journey of self-discovery and growth. By embracing self-love and reframing negative thoughts, you will become more resilient, confident, and empowered to navigate the challenges of life with grace and compassion.

FUTURE

Now, let's talk about the future.

In five years, you will be a young adult, making your way in the world.

Who do you want to be?
What type of person do you want to turn into?

Take a moment to think about your values and what is important to you.

Once you have identified your values, make a plan for how you will stick to them.

It is easy to get swept up in the pressures of society and forget what truly matters to you. But with a clear plan and determination, you can stay true to your values and live a life that is fulfilling and meaningful.

Remember, you are the only one who can make your dreams a reality. Believe in yourself and your capabilities, and never give up on your goals. You have already proven that you are capable of overcoming challenges, and I have no doubt that you will continue to do so in the future.

Who do I want to be?

What type of person do I want to turn into?

What are my values?

What is important to me?

DEVELOPING MY SENSE OF SELF

As we go through life, we accumulate memories and possessions that shape our identity and give us a sense of belonging and purpose. However, it's easy to lose sight of these things as we navigate the challenges and changes that come our way.

In this exercise, I encourage you to make a list of 5 of your favorite objects and describe the memories and emotions that are tied to them. These objects could be from your childhood, your teenage years, or any other significant period of your life. Take a moment to reflect on what role each object has played in your journey of becoming who you are today.

By reconnecting with these objects and the memories they represent, we can gain a deeper understanding of ourselves and our sense of identity. We can also appreciate the people and experiences that have influenced us along the way and feel a greater sense of gratitude and connection.

So let's get started and explore the power of our favorite objects together. Remember, these objects are more than just things – they are symbols of our personal history and the people and experiences that have shaped us. Enjoy the journey of self-discovery!

My favorite objects

☐ _____

☐ _____

☐ _____

☐ _____

☐ _____

MEDITATION

Here is a step-by-step meditation exercise for when you're feeling unworthy and down on yourself:

- Find a quiet and comfortable place where you can sit or lie down without being bothered.

- Take a couple breaths to calm your mind and body.

- Visualize a bright, warm light shining down on you from above.

- Imagine that this light is filled with love and compassion.

- Focus on your breathing, and allow the light to envelop you.

- Imagine that it's washing away all of your negative thoughts and emotions.

As you continue to breathe deeply, repeat the following affirmations to yourself:

I am worthy of love and respect.

I am deserving of happiness and fulfillment.

I am enough, just as I am.

Allow these affirmations to sink in, and notice how they make you feel. If any negative thoughts or emotions come up, acknowledge them, but don't dwell on them. Instead, gently redirect your focus back to the affirmations. Spend as much time as you need in this space of self-love and acceptance.

When you feel ready, slowly bring yourself back to the present moment by taking a few deep breaths.

Remember, it's okay to feel down on yourself sometimes, but it's important to remind yourself that you are worthy of love and respect.

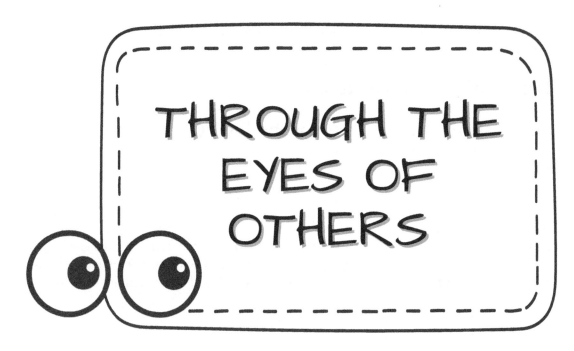

THROUGH THE EYES OF OTHERS

Sometimes, we can be our own worst critics and believe that others perceive us in a negative light.

This negative self-perception can lead to feelings of low self-esteem and self-doubt. However, it's important to remember that our perception of how others see us may not always be accurate.

In this exercise, we will assess our perceptions of how others see us by rating ten statements that others might have on us. This exercise will help us gain insight into how we view ourselves and how we want others to view us, and can ultimately lead to a more positive self-perception.

Take a few deep breaths and try to clear your mind.
Read each statement one at a time, and rate it on a scale from 1 to 8. The scale is as follows:

1: The statement is completely untrue.
2: The statement is mostly untrue.
3: The statement is somewhat untrue.
4: The statement is somewhat true.
5: The statement is mostly true.
6: The statement is completely true, but only sometimes.
7: The statement is completely true most of the time.
8: The statement is completely true all the time.

You are untrustworthy. ☐

You are lazy. ☐

You are selfish. ☐

You are unfriendly. ☐

You are unreliable. ☐

You are rude. ☐

You are insecure. ☐

You are arrogant. ☐

You are insensitive. ☐

You are boring. ☐

Take your time with each statement and be honest with yourself. Try not to judge yourself or feel ashamed of your ratings.

Once you've rated all ten statements, take a step back and look at your ratings as a whole.
Are there any patterns or common themes that you notice?
Do certain statements stand out as being more true or untrue than others?

Remember that just because someone else may perceive you in a certain way doesn't mean it's the truth. You are the only one who truly understands yourself and your intentions.

Use this exercise as an opportunity to reflect on how you see yourself and how you want others to see you.

If there are any statements that you rated as mostly or completely true, think about why that might be and if there are any changes you want to make in your behavior or attitude.

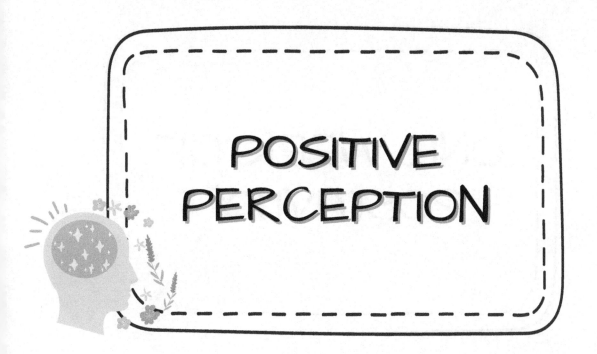

POSITIVE PERCEPTION

In this exercise, you will reflect on how you believe others perceive you in a positive light. Think about qualities or traits that you possess that others admire or appreciate.

Here are some examples of positive statements that others might have on you:

You are a good listener and give thoughtful advice.

You have an amazing sense of humor and always know how to make people laugh.

You are dependable and reliable, always there for others when they need you.

You are intelligent and have a knack for problem-solving.

You are creative and have a unique perspective on the world.

You are kind and compassionate, always putting others' needs before your own.

You are a great friend and always make time for the people in your life.

ONE WEEK OF POSITIVITY

In this chapter, we will explore the power of positive thinking and how it can help you build confidence and nurture self-love. Each day, we will challenge you to write down ten positive things about yourself, your behavior, or what you have accomplished on that day.

We all know that self-love is essential for our overall well-being, but sometimes, it can be challenging to feel good about ourselves. Negative self-talk and criticism can lower our self-esteem and make us feel unworthy. However, positive thinking can help us overcome these negative thoughts and feelings. When we focus on our strengths, accomplishments, and positive traits, we can develop a more positive and healthy self-image.

The exercise of writing down ten positive things about yourself each day might seem daunting at first, but it can have a significant impact on your life.

By actively seeking out positive aspects of yourself and your life, you will start to notice more positive things around you. This will create a cycle of positivity that can help you build confidence and self-love.

DAY 1

- [ ] _____
- [ ] _____
- [ ] _____
- [ ] _____
- [ ] _____
- [ ] _____
- [ ] _____
- [ ] _____
- [ ] _____
- [ ] _____

DAY 2

☐ _____

☐ _____

☐ _____

☐ _____

☐ _____

☐ _____

☐ _____

☐ _____

☐ _____

☐ _____

DAY 3

☐ _____

☐ _____

☐ _____

☐ _____

☐ _____

☐ _____

☐ _____

☐ _____

☐ _____

☐ _____

DAY 4

☐ _____

☐ _____

☐ _____

☐ _____

☐ _____

☐ _____

☐ _____

☐ _____

☐ _____

☐ _____

DAY 5

- [ ] _____
- [ ] _____
- [ ] _____
- [ ] _____
- [ ] _____
- [ ] _____
- [ ] _____
- [ ] _____
- [ ] _____
- [ ] _____

DAY 6

- [ ] _____
- [ ] _____
- [ ] _____
- [ ] _____
- [ ] _____
- [ ] _____
- [ ] _____
- [ ] _____
- [ ] _____
- [ ] _____

DAY 7

- [ ] _____
- [ ] _____
- [ ] _____
- [ ] _____
- [ ] _____
- [ ] _____
- [ ] _____
- [ ] _____
- [ ] _____
- [ ] _____

ACCEPTING COMPLIMENTS

Many of us struggle with accepting compliments, especially as teenagers. We may feel embarrassed or even dismissive when someone says something nice about us, even though we might secretly appreciate the kind words. Learning to accept compliments gracefully is an important part of building a healthy self-image and learning to love ourselves. In this exercise, you will practice receiving compliments and finding different ways to accept them.

Here are five compliments for you to practice with:

1. You have a great sense of humor.
2. You are a talented artist/musician/athlete.
3. You have a kind heart and are always there for your friends.
4. You are intelligent and have a unique perspective on the world.
5. You have a beautiful smile.

Now, think of five different ways you can accept these compliments. You might say "Thank you, that means a lot to me," or "I really appreciate you saying that," or "You just made my day!" Experiment with different responses and find what feels most natural and comfortable for you.

Remember, accepting compliments is not about being arrogant or self-centered, but about acknowledging your own worth and allowing yourself to feel good about who you are.

You have a great sense of humor.
Answer:

You are a talented artist/musician/athlete.
Answer:

You have a kind heart and are always there for your friends.
Answer:

You are intelligent and have a unique perspective on the world.
Answer:

You have a beautiful smile.
Answer:

LEARNING NEW THINGS

KEEP LEARNING

Learning a new skill, such as driving a car, can be challenging and often requires patience and perseverance. Sometimes, you may feel like giving up, but it's important to stay motivated and not let self-doubt get in the way of your progress. One of the ways you can do this is by practicing positive self-talk. In this exercise, you will think about the positive things you have told yourself when you feel like giving up on learning a new skill, such as driving a car.

Exercise:
Think back to a time when you were learning to drive and felt like giving up. What were the negative thoughts that came to mind? Write them down.
Next, reflect on the positive things you told yourself to keep going. Write down at least five positive statements that you can remember saying to yourself.

For each positive statement, reflect on why it was helpful to you. How did it help you keep going? Write down your thoughts.
Finally, think about how you can use positive self-talk in other areas of your life when you feel like giving up. Write down some ideas.

Example:
Negative thoughts: "I'll never get the hang of this. I'm a terrible driver. I should just give up."

Positive self-talk: "I can do this. Everyone starts somewhere. It's okay to make mistakes. I'll get better with practice. I'm proud of myself for trying."
Reflection: When I told myself that I could do it and that it's okay to make mistakes, it helped me feel more confident and motivated to keep trying. It reminded me that learning a new skill takes time and practice, and that it's okay to make mistakes along the way. It also helped me feel proud of myself for trying, even if I didn't get it right the first time.

Using positive self-talk: I can use positive self-talk when I'm feeling discouraged about anything, such as schoolwork or sports. I can remind myself that it's okay to make mistakes and that I'm capable of improving with practice.

NO SELF-DOUBT

Whenever self-doubt and negative thoughts start to creep in, it's important to have strategies to help combat them. One effective method is to engage in positive self-reflection by asking yourself a series of questions.

By focusing on your strengths, accomplishments, and positive qualities, you can dismantle self-doubt and boost your confidence. For teenagers who may be going through a particularly challenging time in their lives, this exercise can be especially helpful.

So, whenever you find yourself struggling with self-doubt, take some time to answer the following questions and remind yourself of all the positive aspects of who you are.

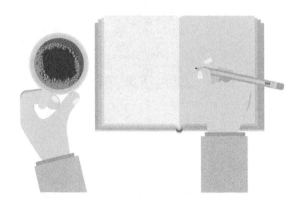

What are some of your past accomplishments that you're proud of?

What are some positive qualities that you possess?

What are some challenges that you have faced and overcome in the past?

What is one thing that you have learned recently that you didn't know before?

What are some things that you enjoy doing and feel confident about?

What are some things that your friends or family members have said about you that make you feel good?

What is one thing that you're curious about or interested in learning more about?

What are some examples of times when you took a risk and it paid off?

What are some ways that you have helped others in the past?

What are some ways that you have grown and developed as a person over time?

CHANGE PERCEPTION

Negative thoughts can have a profound impact on our mental well-being, causing us to feel anxious, stressed, and insecure. One effective way to combat these negative thoughts is to reframe them into more positive and constructive ones. In this exercise, we will focus on reframing negative thoughts to help you build a more positive and confident mindset.

1. *Identify a negative thought that you often have. Write it down in a sentence or two. Example: "I'm not good enough to get into my dream school."*
2. *Reframe the negative thought into a more positive and constructive one. Write it down in a sentence or two. Example: "I have many strengths and qualities that make me a strong candidate for my dream school."*
3. *Repeat the positive thought to yourself several times. Focus on the positive aspects of yourself and your abilities.*
4. *Repeat this exercise for at least five different negative thoughts.*

Examples:

Negative thought: "I always mess up and make mistakes."
Positive reframe: "I am capable of learning from my mistakes and growing from them."

Negative thought: "I will never be as successful as my friends."
Positive reframe: "I am on my own unique path, and my journey may look different from my friends, but that doesn't diminish my own success and accomplishments."

Negative thought: "I'm not pretty enough to be liked by others."
Positive reframe: "My appearance does not define my worth, and I have many positive qualities that make me a likeable person."

Negative thought: "I'll never be able to do that, it's too difficult."
Positive reframe: "I may not be able to do it yet, but with effort and perseverance, I can improve and achieve my goals."

Negative thought: "I'm not smart enough to understand this."
Positive reframe: "I may not understand it right away, but with effort and dedication, I can learn and gain a better understanding."

Now practice by reframing your own negative thoughts when they arise:

Negative thought:
Positive reframe:

Negative thought:
Positive reframe:

Negative thought:
Positive reframe:

Negative thought:
Positive reframe:

Negative thought:
Positive reframe:

Negative thought:
Positive reframe:

Negative thought:
Positive reframe:

Negative thought:
Positive reframe:

Negative thought:
Positive reframe:

Adult: Self-love Unlocked

Congratulations on reaching this point in your journey! You've worked hard to get here and have learned how to love and accept yourself. It's a remarkable accomplishment that should be celebrated.

In this chapter, we'll be focusing on the importance of maintaining and nourishing the love you have for yourself. You've done the hard work of unlocking your self-love, but it's crucial to understand that self-love is not a one-time event. It's a continuous process that requires constant maintenance and effort.

Many people believe that once they've reached a certain level of self-love, they no longer need to work on it. However, this is far from the truth. You must continue to practice self-love exercises and maintain a healthy relationship with yourself to avoid losing the progress you've made.

So, continue reading, and let's work together to ensure that you don't lose the self-love you've worked so hard to achieve.

LETTER TO MYSELF

Congratulations on making it this far! You have faced so many challenges and obstacles, yet here you are, still standing. I am proud of you for everything you have accomplished and for the person you have become.

As you write this letter to yourself, I want you to take a moment to show yourself some compassion. Acknowledge your struggles and remind yourself that it is okay to make mistakes. Remember that you are strong and capable of overcoming anything that comes your way.

MY FAVORITE ACTIVITIES

With the demands of school, work, and other responsibilities, it's easy to overlook the things that bring us joy and relaxation. However, taking time to engage in our favorite activities can help us to reduce stress, improve our mood, and enhance our overall well-being.

In this exercise, I encourage you to choose a different favorite activity every day for 7 days and write down how you feel afterwards. This could be anything from reading a book, to going for a walk, to trying a new hobby. The key is to prioritize your own enjoyment and make time for the things that make you feel happy and fulfilled.

By making a conscious effort to include our favorite activities in our weekly schedule, we can cultivate a sense of balance and purpose in our lives. It's easy to get caught up in the daily routine and forget to take care of ourselves, but by taking time for the things we love, we can replenish our energy and increase our productivity in other areas of our lives.
So let's get started and explore the power of our favorite activities together.

DAY 1

Favorite Activity:

How it made me feel:

_____

_____

_____

_____

_____

_____

_____

_____

_____

_____

_____

_____

_____

_____

DAY 2

Favorite Activity:

How it made me feel:

_____

_____

_____

_____

_____

_____

_____

_____

_____

_____

_____

_____

_____

DAY 3

Favorite Activity:

How it made me feel:

_____

_____

_____

_____

_____

_____

_____

_____

_____

_____

_____

_____

DAY 4

Favorite Activity:

How it made me feel:

_____

_____

_____

_____

_____

_____

_____

_____

_____

_____

_____

_____

DAY 5

Favorite Activity:

How it made me feel:

DAY 6

Favorite Activity:

How it made me feel:

_____

_____

_____

_____

_____

_____

_____

_____

_____

_____

_____

_____

_____

DAY 7

Favorite Activity:

How it made me feel:
_____

_____

_____

_____

_____

_____

_____

_____

_____

_____

_____

_____

_____

BUILDING HEALTHY HABITS

Developing healthy habits is an essential part of any self-love journey. Healthy habits help us feel good physically, mentally, and emotionally, and can have a positive impact on our overall well-being.

In this exercise, we will focus on creating positive long-term habits that will help you feel your best and support your journey towards self-love.

Step 1: Identify the habits you want to establish.
Take a few moments to reflect on the habits you want to establish. These could include things like exercising regularly, eating nutritious meals, getting enough sleep, practicing mindfulness or meditation, spending time with friends and family, or pursuing hobbies that bring you joy. Write down a list of the habits you want to establish.

Step 2: Create a plan.
Developing healthy habits takes time and effort, so it's important to create a plan that works for you. Start by choosing one or two habits to focus on at a time. Then, create a plan for how you will establish and maintain these habits. Consider things like when and where you will practice your habit, any resources or tools you will need, and what obstacles you may face.

Step 3: Start small.

It's important to start small when creating new habits. This can help you build momentum and establish a strong foundation for success. For example, if you want to start exercising regularly, you could begin by committing to 10 minutes of activity per day and gradually increase your time over time.

Step 4: Track your progress.

Tracking your progress can help you stay motivated and accountable. Consider using a habit tracker or journal to record your progress and celebrate your successes along the way.

Step 5: Adjust as needed.

Creating new habits can be challenging, and it's important to be flexible and adjust your plan as needed. If you encounter obstacles or setbacks, don't give up! Instead, reevaluate your plan and make adjustments as needed.

Step 6: Practice self-compassion.

Remember that developing healthy habits takes time and effort. Be kind to yourself, practice self-compassion, and celebrate your progress along the way.

Developing healthy habits is an essential part of any self-love journey. By prioritizing our physical, mental, and emotional well-being, we show ourselves love and care. Healthy habits can help us feel more energized, reduce stress and anxiety, improve our mood, and build self-confidence. When we take care of ourselves, we also set an example for others to do the same, creating a positive ripple effect in our communities. So, take the time to establish healthy habits that support your self-love journey, and watch as you flourish and thrive.

HABIT 1

Build your own healthy habits:

Step 1: Identify the habits you want to establish.

Describe the habit you want to establish:

Step 2: Create a plan.

Write a step-by-step plan to accomplish this:

Step 3: Start small.

Daily commitment time:

Step 4: Track your progress.

Write a mark for each day in which you practiced the healthy habit:

Step 6: Practice self-compassion.

Write self-compassion notes for yourself throughout the process:

HABIT 2

Build your own healthy habits:

Step 1: Identify the habits you want to establish.

Describe the habit you want to establish:

Step 2: Create a plan.

Write a step-by-step plan to accomplish this:

Step 3: Start small.

Daily commitment time:

Step 4: Track your progress.

Write a mark for each day in which you practiced the healthy habit:

Step 6: Practice self-compassion.

Write self-compassion notes for yourself throughout the process:

HABIT 3

Build your own healthy habits:

Step 1: Identify the habits you want to establish.

Describe the habit you want to establish:

Step 2: Create a plan.

Write a step-by-step plan to accomplish this:

Step 3: Start small.

Daily commitment time:

Step 4: Track your progress.

Write a mark for each day in which you practiced the healthy habit:

Step 6: Practice self-compassion.

Write self-compassion notes for yourself throughout the process:

HABIT 4

Build your own healthy habits:

Step 1: Identify the habits you want to establish.

Describe the habit you want to establish:

Step 2: Create a plan.

Write a step-by-step plan to accomplish this:

Step 3: Start small.

Daily commitment time:

Step 4: Track your progress.

Write a mark for each day in which you practiced the healthy habit:

Step 6: Practice self-compassion.

Write self-compassion notes for yourself throughout the process:

HABIT 5

Build your own healthy habits:

Step 1: Identify the habits you want to establish.

Describe the habit you want to establish:

Step 2: Create a plan.

Write a step-by-step plan to accomplish this:

Step 3: Start small.

Daily commitment time:

Step 4: Track your progress.

Write a mark for each day in which you practiced the healthy habit:

Step 6: Practice self-compassion.

Write self-compassion notes for yourself throughout the process:

As you come to the end of this book on self-love, I hope you've learned that just like growing a tree from a seed, your journey to self-love takes time and effort, but it's worth it. You've discovered how to practice positive thinking, build confidence, and eliminate self-doubt, and even build healthier habits to become a better person and feel happier with yourself.

Remember that self-love isn't a one-time event but a journey that lasts a lifetime. As you continue to love yourself, you'll unlock the full potential of who you are and who you can become. You'll be able to set boundaries, follow your passions, and accomplish your goals. You'll also attract more positive and fulfilling relationships into your life.

Self-love is essential to your success in life, both now and in the future. When you love yourself, you'll be more resilient and better equipped to face life's challenges. You'll be able to handle criticism and rejection without taking them personally. You'll also be able to bounce back from setbacks and learn from your mistakes.

I hope that the lessons you've learned in this book will stay with you for a lifetime. Remember that you are worthy of love and respect, and that you can accomplish anything you set your mind to as long as you believe in yourself. Keep growing, keep learning, and keep loving yourself every step of the way.

With love and encouragement,
Bella Clark

Made in the USA
Las Vegas, NV
09 February 2024

85570370R00059